James and His Weird Mad

God's Hope for Children of Divorce

WRITTEN BY

KELLI DIONNE

Copyright © 2023

ILLUSTRATED BY

ERIN DOUGHERTY

For all children of divorce needing hope for the future.

Scripture quotations are from The Holy Bible, English Standard Version, copyright © 2008, by Crossway.

Divorce is a painful, difficult, and confusing situation for children. Adult decisions and choices are made, and children are swept into circumstances that they would not choose for themselves. Sadly, this suffering is becoming common this side of heaven, even in God's church.

This book shows children that the God of the Bible is the one that they need with this kind of suffering. It isn't intended to solve every problem or answer every question, but through the eyes and ears of a young boy, children can learn that God really does care about this pain, and this child, and has the answers in His word. My desire is that it will be an opportunity for you to have continued conversations about the sovereignty, compassion, faithfulness, and power of God with children who are angry, sad, and confused about drastic changes taking place in their families and lives.

We needed a resource for young children in the biblical counseling world on this topic, and I wrote something I could use with the children I counsel at Faith Biblical Counseling Center in Spokane, Washington. Our church is an ACBC (Association of Certified Biblical Counselors) training center, and our desire is to equip biblical counselors to serve hurting people. I pray this resource will help you minister truth and grace to the children in your environments.

Now more than ever the church needs to serve hurting children as our culture continues to rebel against God. The church of Christ is key to help families who are hurting by sharing Christ's love and truth. We have an opportunity to tell children that Jesus is the one they need, that they are loved, and will be helped. We must say, "We love you, and we want you to know that God loves you and promises to help."

This book provides a foundation to help parents and helpers continue to have these conversations with their children instead of going to outside sources for help for their family. This is a pivotal time to serve young children so that, even though the problem of divorce might not be solved this side of eternity, God's comfort and truth from Scripture will be their hope throughout all the days of their lives. May we not neglect this opportunity.

For God's praise,
Kelli Dionne, MABC
Faith Bible Church
Spokane, WA
angryjameshope@gmail.com

Find James and His Weird Mad at Amazon.com.

Special thanks to: Ben Palpant for your encouragement and guidance and Lana Pustovit for your servant's heart and expertise.

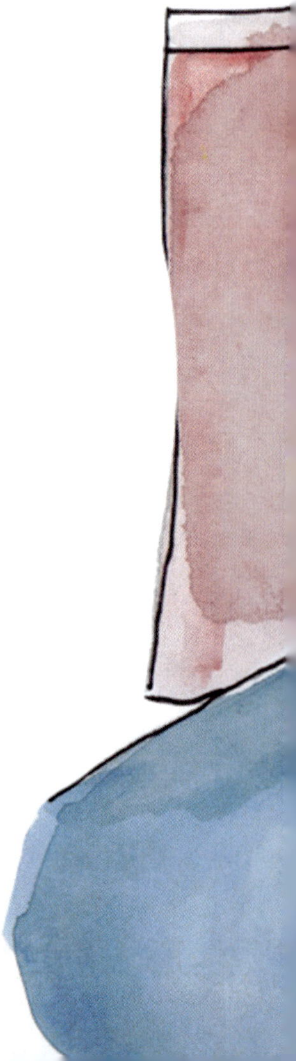

James woke up Friday morning at his grandparents' house. His stomach felt weird. His chest felt tight. Today was supposed to be a great day. He was going to his dad's house for a sleepover.

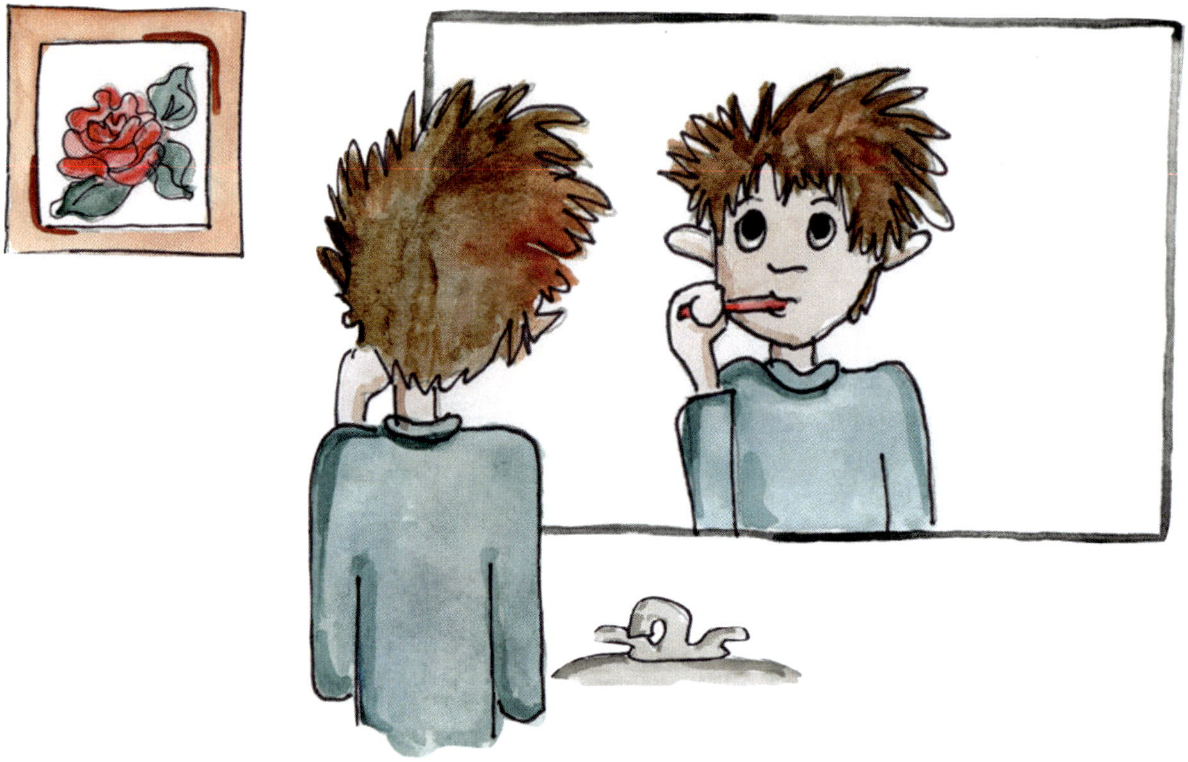

It didn't feel great.
It felt...weird.

The more James thought about it, the sadder he got.
"Why is this happening to me?"

The grownups had been saying, "Your parents still love you, and they always will. They just don't love each other anymore. But don't worry. You will be okay."

But, that morning, all James could say to himself was, "I feel weird, and I don't think I'm okay."

It wasn't having the sleepover that was the problem.

He liked staying with Grandma and Grandpa Thursday nights when Mom worked late, but something about going to his dad's new house felt...strange.

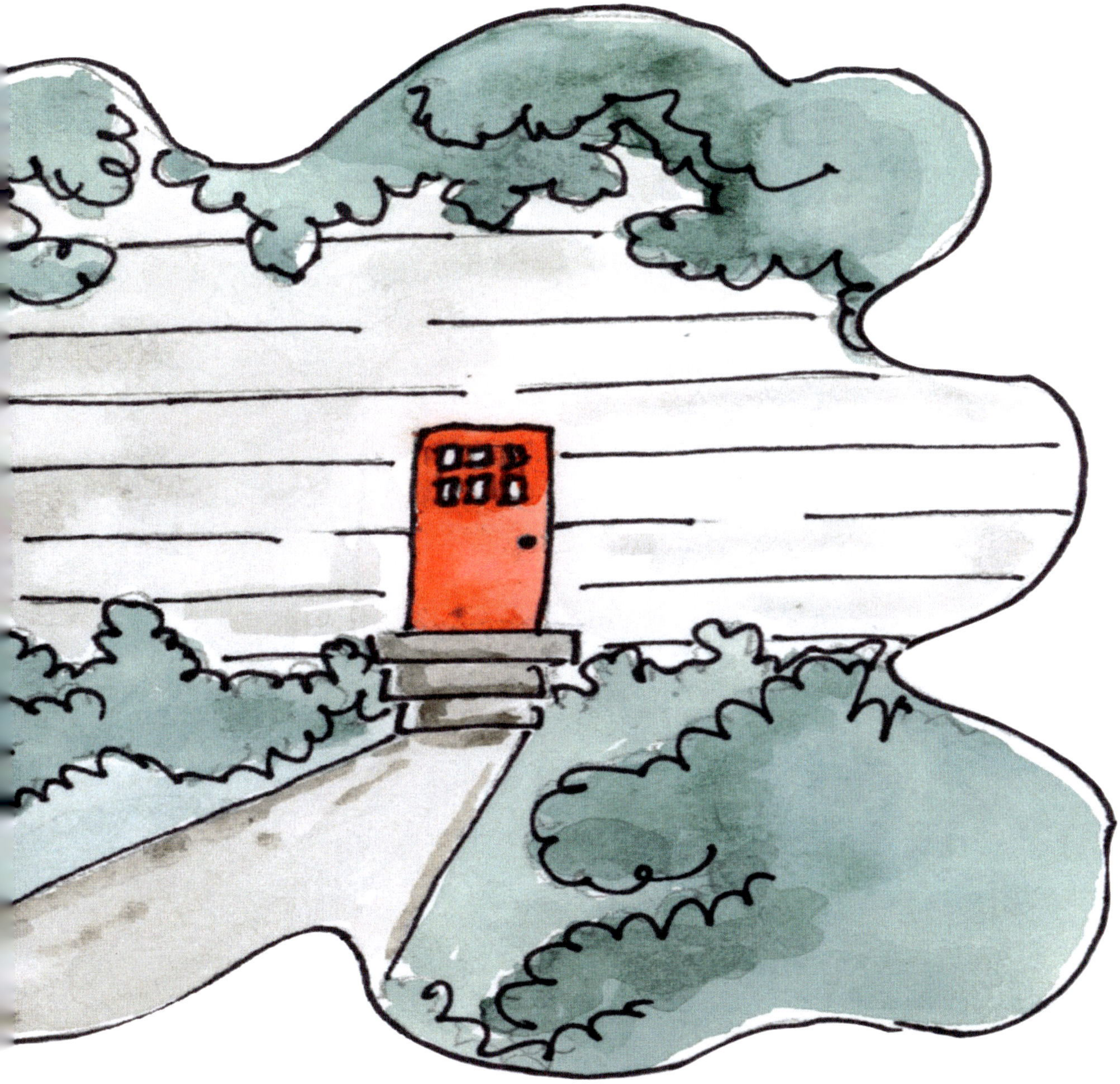

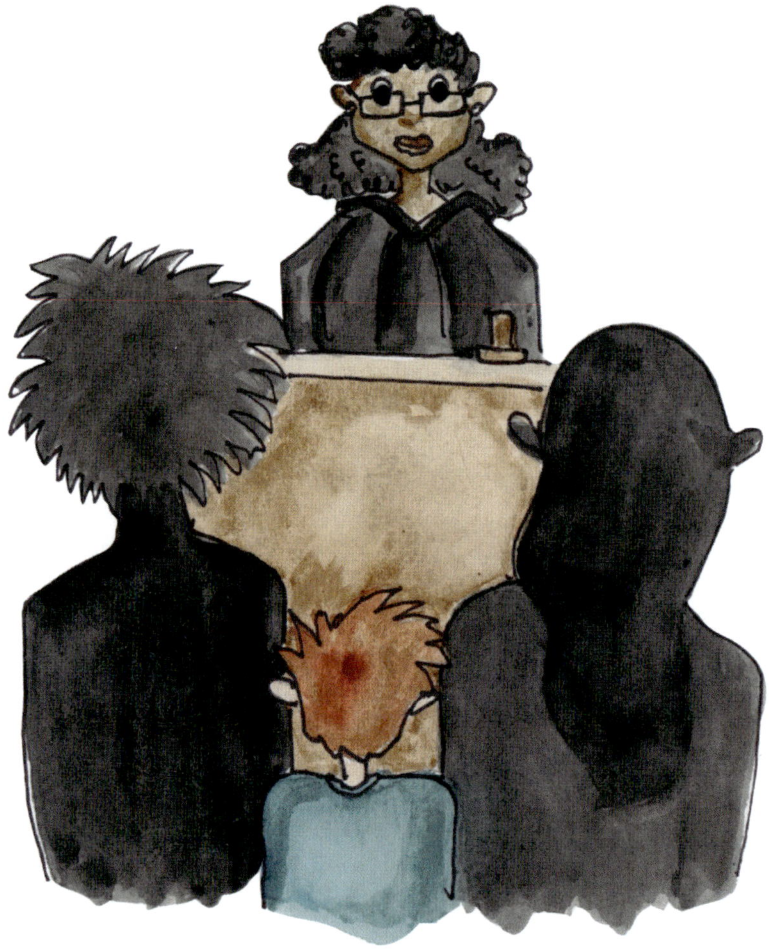

Last week, he had to go to a grown-up place where an old lady in a black robe said he'd be okay. She was sorry about what was happening to him and wanted to help him.

She sent him to see another lady for talking. That lady told him stuff about grown-up choices not being a kid's fault. She told him he would feel better if he made his own good choices.

"Wait," thought James that day. "I'm a kid! I don't know how to make good choices! I want my PARENTS to make good choices!"

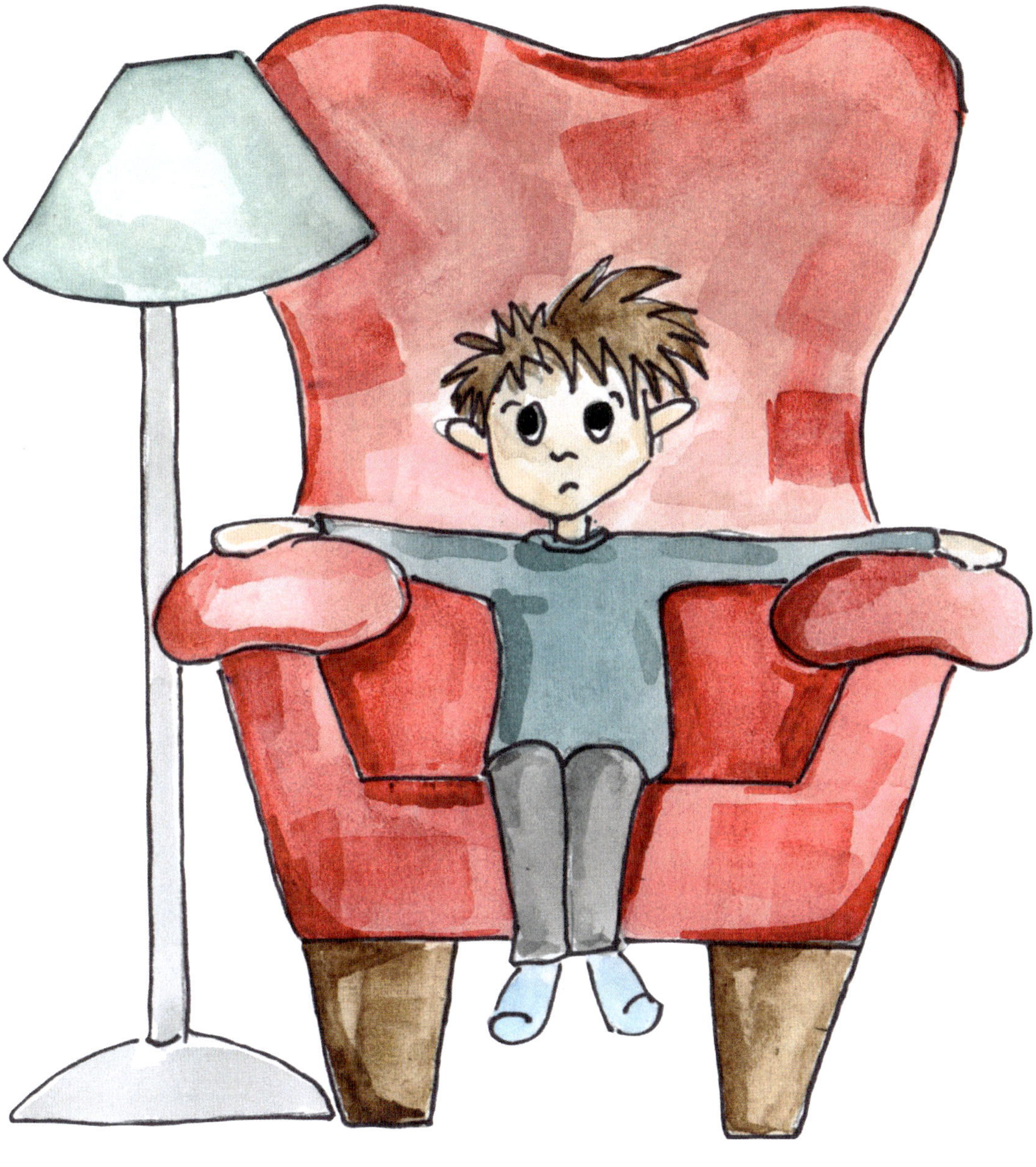

Remembering the black-robe lady and the talking lady made James feel terrible.

Mom and Dad didn't make good choices, at least, James didn't think so.

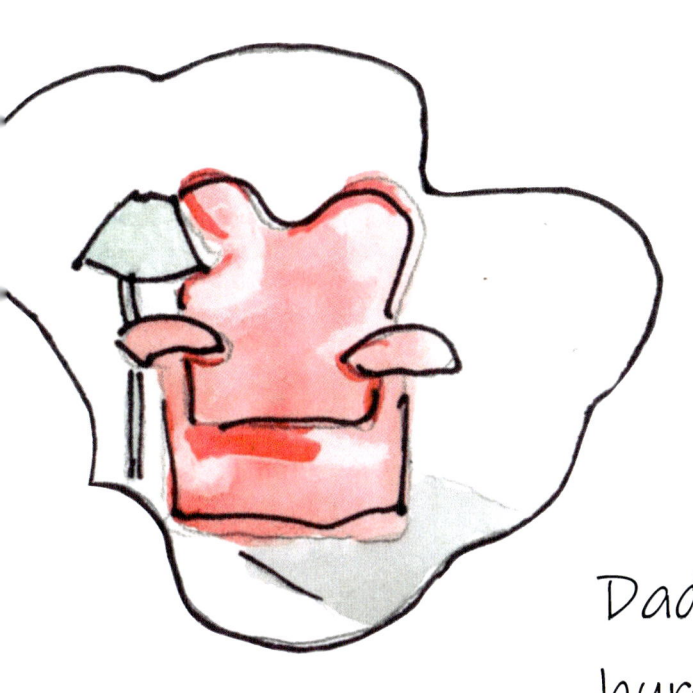

Dad made a choice that hurt Mom, and Mom made a choice to not let him live with her. Those choices seemed like bad ones to James.

James thought, "I don't want to go to Dad's. I want him to make a good choice and come home to me."

His chest felt really tight, and he wasn't hungry at all. Maybe, just maybe, Grandma and Grandpa could help. When he was at their house, he had fun. They had toys, books, and treats.

It wasn't his house, where he wanted his parents to be forever, but it was pretty great. At the breakfast table, they noticed James was quiet.

Grandpa said, "Hey, buddy, how are you feeling today?"

James got more worried. All the grown-ups had said he would be fine. Did Grandma and Grandpa think so, too? Would they think he was dumb because he didn't feel fine? Would they think he was being a baby?

He decided to make a choice. He decided to tell them how he felt.

"I feel weird. My stomach feels sick. My chest feels hard. I'm not happy…"

"I'm mad!"

"I'm so mad!"

"I'm so, so,
so mad!"

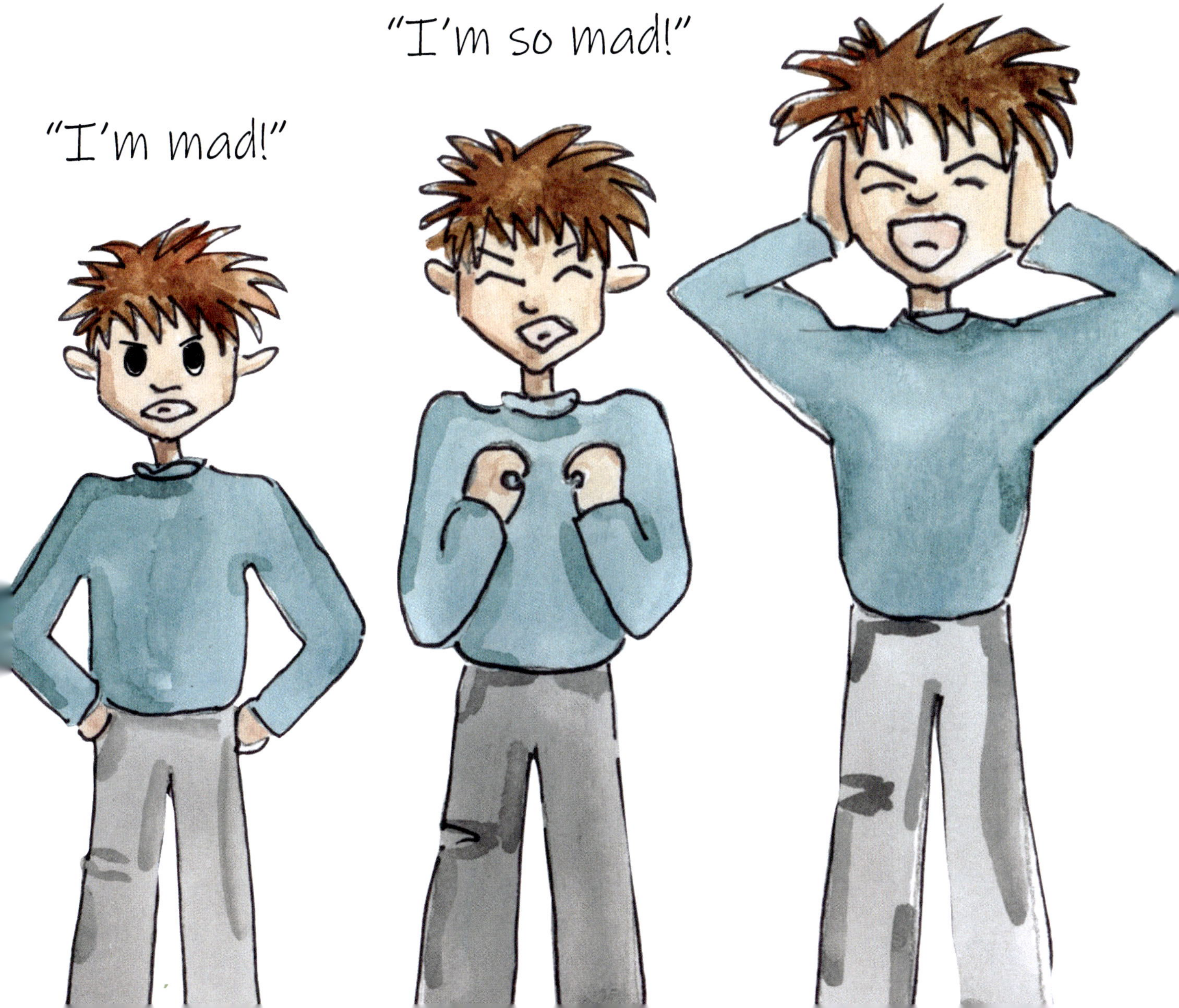

Grandma and Grandpa came to him and hugged him, and Grandpa asked, "Can you tell us about your mad?"

James was nervous. They were Dad's parents. Would they be hurt by his mad? James loved them a lot, and he knew they loved him. He also knew they loved Jesus.

So, he made a choice... to talk.

"I don't want to go to Dad's today. I want Dad to come home. I want him to love Mom right and take care of us. I want Mom to let him come home. Everyone says Mom and Dad still love me and that things will be okay, but nothing feels okay to me."

Grandma and Grandpa had big tears rolling down their cheeks. James got big tears, too. Grandma was the first to talk.

"James, we are so, so, so sad about this. You are right. This isn't okay! This is horrible! We love you, and we want to help you. Grandpa and I always try to solve our problems by talking to Jesus. We want to understand things the way He wants us to, so we see what he says in his word, the Bible. You know that, don't you?"

James knew that.

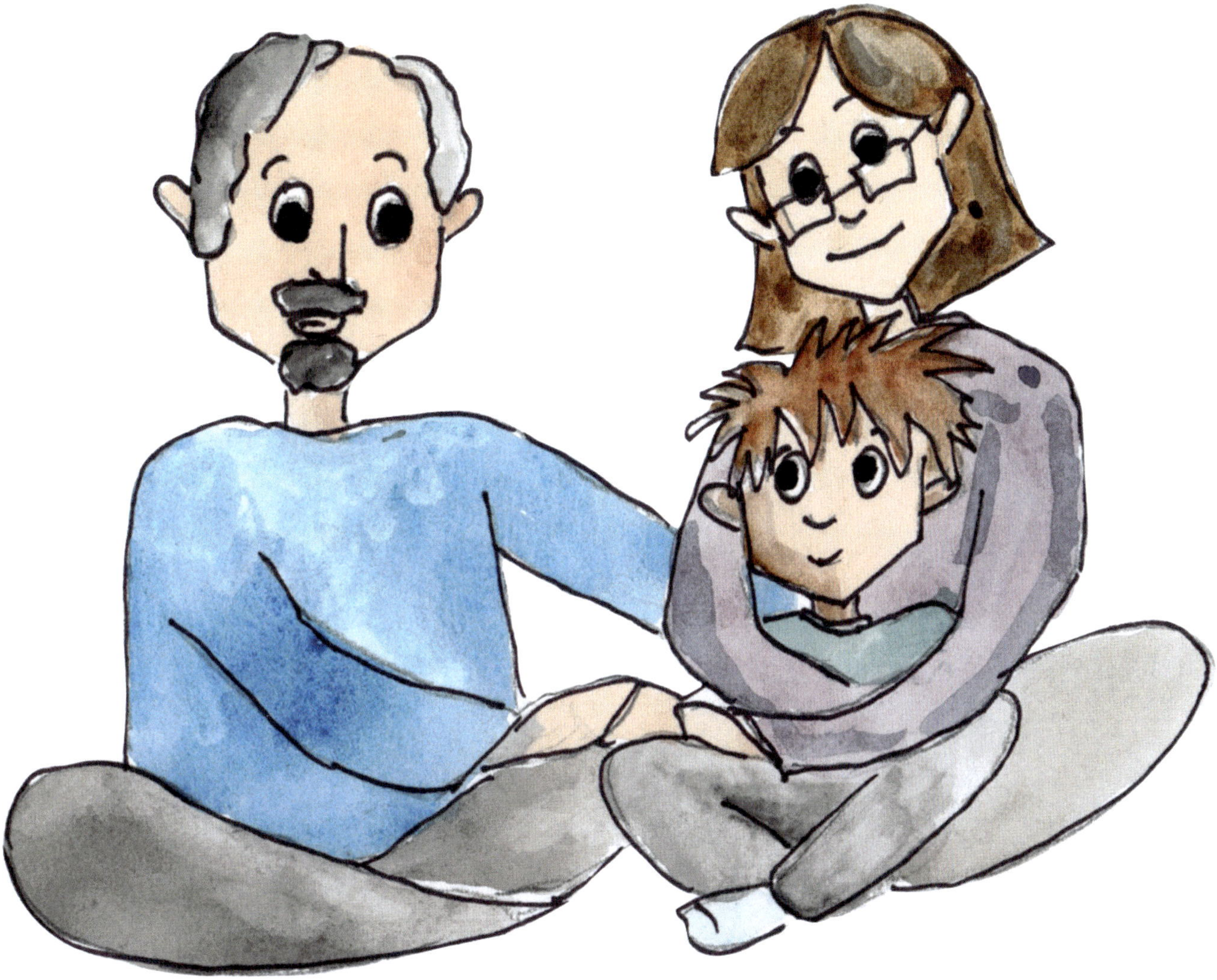

Grandma went on, "Jesus loves us, and marriage is a way for us to show that to the world. Divorce isn't part of God's good plan. It happens because of sin."

James said, "Oh, I know what sin is. Sin is when people make wrong choices."

"That's right," Grandpa said. "I don't know if you know this, but my parents got divorced when I was a kid. It was hard! I came to know that when a couple gets divorced, they make the best choices that they can, but they aren't always right. Sometimes their kids get very hurt by those choices. When that happens, kids feel very sad. I felt very sad."

"Is that why my stomach and chest feel weird?"

"Yes, James. Our bodies often remind us that we hurt on the inside. This might hurt for a long time."

James gulped. "All the grown-ups say I'll be okay because my parents still love me even though they don't love each other."

"Well," Grandpa said, "that's true. They aren't lying to you about that. They want to help. But, the real truth is you will only feel better when Jesus helps you feel better. As you get to know Him, life makes a little more sense."

"How does that happen?" asked James.

Grandma said, "The way God does this is a big idea, but we think you can get it. Do you?" James thought so.

Grandpa began, "I had to learn that bad things happen in this world every day. When they do it is easy to think that life will always be bad. You know, there is a boy in the Bible who had very bad things happen to him...
Lots of bad things."

"His brothers hated him."
"He was thrown into a pit!"
"He was sold into slavery."
"He was lied about and put in jail."
(Genesis 43-50)

James was shocked that a story like that was in the Bible! He said, "I bet his stomach and chest felt awful!"

Grandpa continued, "No matter what happened to him, the boy always thought about God and tried to please Him. God used him to help a ton of people when he grew up! One day, God made a way for him to tell the people who hurt him that even though they made wrong choices, God still did something good in his life."

"His name was Joseph. God taught Joseph many things during his very hard time and kept him close to himself. Joseph only felt better when he stayed close to God and trusted him."

"Wow...That seems like a VERY BIG IDEA!" said James.

"You're right, buddy," Grandpa answered, "but even a big idea can be understood with God's big help. God's big help comes from knowing Him, through His word in the Bible, and from staying close to Him, with the help of Jesus."

James thought for a moment.
"I think I get some of that, you guys. The big problem is, I still feel weird, and I'm still mad!"

Grandma said, "We feel weird and mad, too. Another part of the big idea is that divorce hurts. Always. It's not part of God's good plan and we won't ever feel good about it. We must talk to our weird feelings with the truth we learn from the Bible."

"You might never feel good about some of the choices your parents made, but you have someone who knows everything. Jesus will always help you, and His love can help you feel better, even when nothing else can."

"One of my favorite verses is Matthew 11:28-30, 'Come to me, all who labor and are heavy laden and I will give you rest. Take my yoke upon you, and learn from me, for I am gentle and lowly in heart, and you will find rest for your souls. For my yoke is easy and my burden is light.'"

Grandpa shared, "James, my favorite Bible verse says, 'You (God) will keep in perfect peace those whose minds are steadfast, because they trust in you.' "(Isaiah 26:3)

"When I think about God, I have peace. That peace helps me feel better. Could we pray and ask God to help you keep your mind on Him and give you peace? He knows the mad and weird you are feeling. He promises to help, and He will. We will help you, too. We can trust Jesus together." *

James smiled. His chest felt a little softer. He decided to ask God for help.

*Christians know that children need the gospel for life to make sense, and to be able to really trust God. This is a helpful resource for continued conversation: "Leading Your Child to Christ: Biblical Direction for Sharing the Gospel" by Marty Machowski

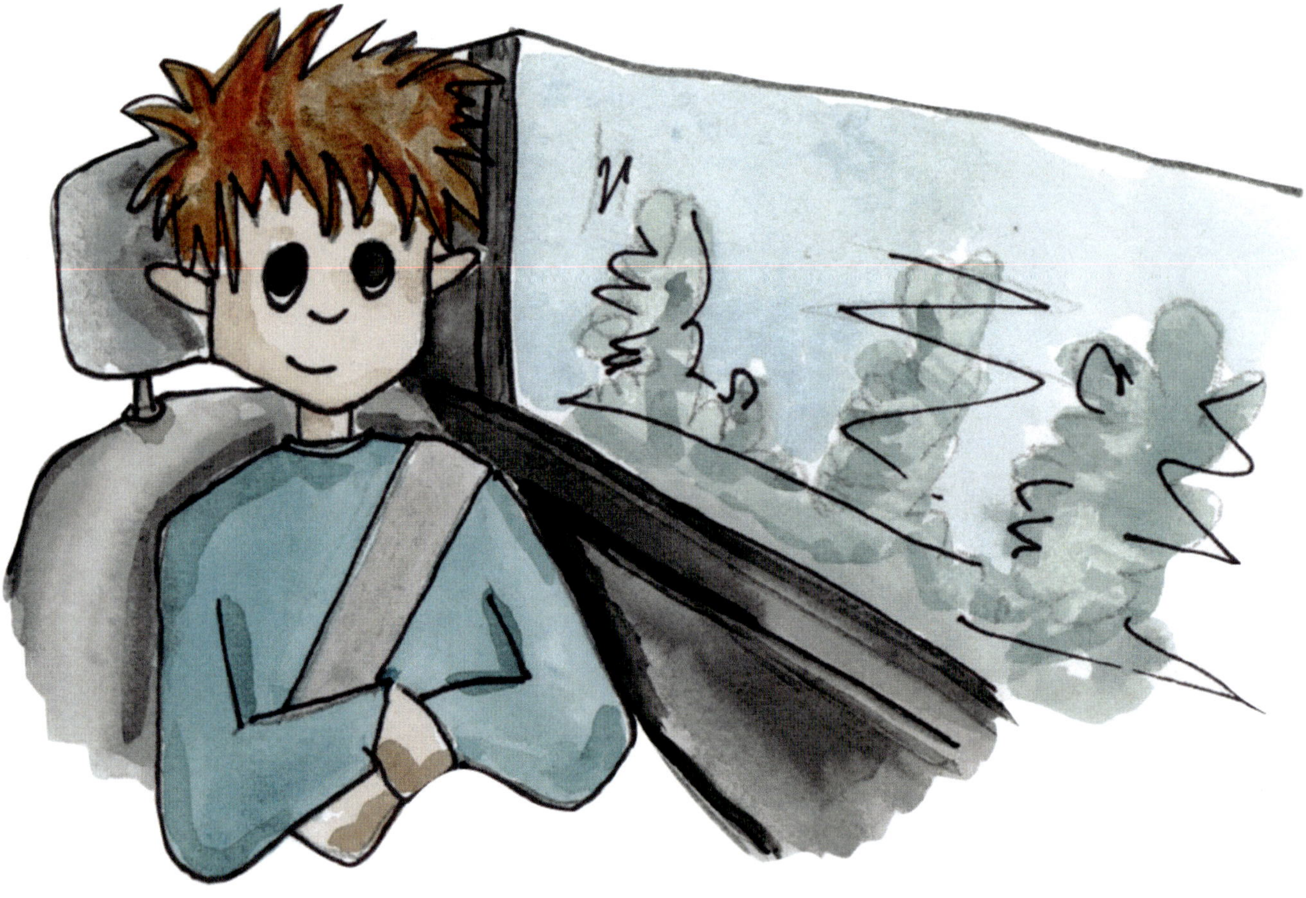

That night in the car with Dad, James looked out the window and thought about what he had learned earlier that day.

He thought about Joseph and how God had helped him. He wondered how God could help him too, but he knew Grandma and Grandpa believed God could. James didn't have everything figured out, but he made a choice to ask God for help. He prayed quietly as Dad drove. He didn't know everything, but he knew God was real, and with God's help, things just might get better.

Trusting God felt like the best choice for him. (1 Peter 5:7)

Made in the USA
Las Vegas, NV
17 May 2024